Under sail

Und

Photography & text
Gilles Martin-Raget

er sail

HACHETTE
Illustrated

Contents

Introduction

The joy of sailing

For the past twenty years I have had the honour, pleasure and privilege of photographing the sea and the men, women and vessels that sail on it. Why did I decide to specialize in this type of photography? Quite simply because I love the sea – I love being at sea, being aware of its presence, seeing it, touching it and riding its waves.

But I never forget that, for many professional sailors, going to sea is primarily a duty, an obligation, since the sea is their place of work. The idea of deriving pleasure from it might therefore be thought frivolous (especially by those who work and risk their lives at sea), given the many maritime tragedies and disasters that have taken place over the centuries.

That said, I count myself extremely lucky to be able to practice my profession as a photographer at sea, or sometimes quite literally above it when I am taking aerial photographs.

It is impossible to describe in simple terms the joy of being at sea. It is a complex mixture of emotions born of a wide range of experiences, from peace and tranquillity, through joy and elation, to the exhaustion and anguish of more difficult and dangerous moments. But it should always be borne in mind that the sea is not man's natural environment – he is merely tolerated and allowed to move within its confines. Sailors and their vessels must weather the storms and survive the hardships unleashed upon them by the elements.

The pages that follow offer only a limited selection of the most powerful images I have experienced over the years, images that I have been inspired, at one time or another, to capture on film.

It is an all-too-brief summary of the extraordinary moments and exceptional events I have been privileged to witness, of the sailors, celebrated and unknown, I have had the honour of meeting and of the boats, both large and small, ordinary and prestigious, I have had the pleasure of seeing under sail.

It has been my overriding ambition to capture these images, recording these incredible moments and unusual situations, many of which occur far out at sea, so that those who were not there can share the joy of being at sea.

Gilles Martin-Raget
Port-Man

Pages 6/7
Breaker on the coral-reef lagoon surrounding the island of Raiatea, French Polynesia.

Pages 8/9
The lighthouse at the entrance to Les Sables-d'Olonne harbour, on the date set for the departure of the Vendée Globe 1999–2000. The event was postponed until the storm had subsided.

Pages 10/11
A small water-spout blown up by the wind on the island of Uahine, French Polynesia.

< Crew members sitting out have a front-seat view of the spectacle created by light, wind and waves.

The passion for racing

It all starts at the age of five or six when you're taken out for the first time in a small sailing dinghy or a huge 470 and told to sit still, wearing a life jacket that's far too big for you and prevents you seeing what's happening beyond the gunwale. All you can see is water flashing by in the wind and water sloshing about in the bottom of the boat. Everything is alarming – the movement, the noise, the spray. Are we going to capsize? But then you begin to get used to it, and even to enjoy it, and, as you go more often, you earn the right to hold the jib sheet and, later, sit in the trapeze until one day you're allowed to take the helm. Now it won't be long before you start racing since, inevitably, you have gradually become obsessed – you want to go faster than the next boat, manoeuvre more quickly than the next crew, make the best tacks. You are getting tired of sailing round in circles and you'll soon be competing in a club race. Too late, you're hooked!

From then, on it's just the size and shape – and possibly the price – of your boat that changes. Young enthusiasts in sailing-dinghies, champions preparing for the Olympics, fanatics who race round three buoys, lovers of one-design sailboats and cruise-yachts, experts on match-racing and ocean-racing yachtsmen, fierce defenders of monohull racing yachts and devotees of multihulls, billionaires hooked on sailing and able to equip and race a maxi in the most prestigious races in the world – all share the same passion. They all want to cross the finish line first, to be part of the chaos and excitement of the start, they all appreciate good tacking and applaud winning tactics, they enthuse about an unconventional turn around a buoy and fear a risky off-course manoeuvre/exit from the course course exit. Some like to sail close to the wind, others prefer a fair wind, some like calm weather, others are happy only when the wind is whipping up the spray and blowing through the rigging. Masters of manoeuvre, crack crews, acclaimed helmsmen, determined navigators, anxious owners – all share the same love for the sea, the wind and waves, and take in their stride the problems posed by the uncontrollable elements, which are a fundamental part of their passion.

< A close encounter between two 49ers (fortyniners) during the series world championship at Bandol in 2000. This finely balanced little yacht, designed by former Australian Olympic champion Julian Besthwaite for the Sydney 2000 Olympic Games, is the most advanced version of those racing yachts known as dinghies. It is above all an over-rigged bomb that makes great physical demands on the crew. A 49er under sail is always a spectacular sight.

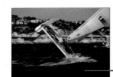

21 Will it or won't it? Sailing is first and foremost a question of balance. The point of no return appears to have been reached by this over-rigged catamaran designed for the Trophée Clairefontaine, the famous French regatta whose races are run close to the shore and can be watched at first hand by the general public. This demonstration circuit and the races for Australian 18-footers (5.5 metres) are the latest initiatives in the field since sailing is not an ideal spectator sport. The rules are complex, there may be no wind and there are not many stretches of water that allow large yachts to sail close to the shore. However, there are a few exceptions, for example Cowes, St Tropez, Sydney and Marseilles, where this photograph was taken. Incredible as it may seem, this catamaran helmed by Yvan Bourgnon finally 'fell on its feet'!

17 A 470 'planing'. Many great champions made their racing debut on board this sailing dinghy designed by Olympic yachtsman Jean-Jacques Herbulot. It has also helped thousands of young people to master the art of sailing and discover the joys of 'planing', demonstrated here by Jean-François Cuzon and Benoît Petit during the Semaine Olympique Française (French Olympic Week) held annually at Hyères. As it gathers speed, the boat's flat bottom enables the hull to hydroplane. The crew sits in the stern to keep the bow up and prevent it ploughing through the water. Sitting on the caisson, the helmsman negotiates the waves while the second crew member trims the spinnaker. It's fast and exhilarating, and good reflexes are needed to stop the boat taking off. But don't forget to breathe or you'll get cramps!

23 Match racing in the shadow of the Sydney Opera House. This type of yacht racing, a legacy of the America's Cup, involves only two boats competing in a one-on-one duel. The object is not to finish in the fastest time but to cross the finish line before your opponent. All forms of tactics and strategy are allowed, which led to the introduction of direct umpiring to avoid endless wrangles between umpires and competitors over contentious rights of way. Match racing is becoming increasingly popular and has its own circuit and permanent rankings. For the most skilled competitors, it's a springboard to gain a place at the helm in an America's Cup team.

19 The bow of a Soling, a three-man keelboat, is a joy to watch as it cleaves elegantly through the waves. Lightweight racing champions spend days training at sea, in all seasons and often until late in the evening, like this crew sailing in Hyères harbour in mid-January.

The passion for racing

Danish champion Paul Elvström (left) has won the most awards in the history of lightweight racing. He has become an inspiration to such up-and-coming young champions as windsurfing gold medallist Christopher Zieber (right).

< 'Bootherie', a technique invented by Australian champion Mitch Booth, is used when sailing a Tornado before the wind. It involves a crew member standing on the hull on the lee side so as to raise the other hull and thereby increase the speed.

∧ Sailing at full speed under spinnaker, a 49er (fortyniner) can reach 20 plus knots. Watch out for unexpected course exits.

∧ Veering wildly round buoys, being drenched by flying spray, raising the centreboard and jostling for position on the start line are just a few of the joys of top-level lightweight racing. These events require not only physical skill, fitness and quick reactions but also the mental agility necessary continually to assess the wind, trim the sails and modify tactics and strategy.

 **29** Looking for wind in the Baie de Quiberon during the Spi Ouest-France regatta. Along with Kieler Woche (Kiel Week) in Germany and Cowes Week in England, the Spi Ouest-France, held at Easter, is one of the major European regattas for monotypes and cruisers. In the evening, the 500 or so yachts crowd into the little Breton port of Trinité-sur-Mer. Competitors are divided into three race areas and compete in two categories – compensated time for cruisers and real time for monotypes (one-design sailboats). These regattas enable occasional racers to compete on board yachts that they cruise on regularly.

 **27** Speeds of 30 plus knots can be reached by the Hobie T22, the most exciting one-design class ever produced. It is a direct legacy of the 'speed machine' *Long Shot*, which held the sailing speed record for several years. The T22 can take a two-man crew and has truly amazing acceleration, more like a car than a yacht. It has two hulls, two windsurfing masts, two hydrofoils, an auxiliary rudder and bow skids that act as sensors and automatically adjust the fore-and-aft trim. The 'helmsman' lies in the central hull like the pilot of a single-seater and uses his feet to steer the rudder bar. The T22 has not been widely available but those who have tried it out will never forget the experience.

 **31** Maxi yachts, spinnakers straining toward the finish, compete in the Rolex Cup at Porto Cervo in Sardinia. These 80-foot (25-metre) giants are the longest – and therefore the most expensive – racing yachts in the world, but their size invests them with a certain presence that is akin to beauty. They are sophisticated craft, manned by a crew of more than twenty since, despite the extremely complex and mainly hydraulic deck equipment, there is always a need for lots of muscle power to manage the huge sails, some of which can be as stiff as cardboard. Beautiful and majestic when set, these sails become unmanageable monsters when lowered onto the deck.

The passion for racing

 33 In close company during the One Ton Cup 2000 in Marseilles. One-design yacht races – here IC 45s – have the merit of putting competitors on an equal footing in terms of equipment and so better display the skill of the crews. However, this restriction doesn't apply to the sails, which can be of any size, shape and material. The art of the master sail makers lies in making them as light, resilient and propulsive as possible, especially the spinnakers, whose panels are no longer sewn but glued together. The flat sails used to sail against the wind are now heat moulded.

On board a racing yacht: trimming the sails; manoeuvres on the forecastle; chatting while sitting out.

< Lowering the spinnaker on board the maxi yacht Inspiration. It takes a good deal of muscle, organization, speed and 'puff' to get a sail measuring up to 600 square yards (500 m²) into the hold and then into its case. In rough weather, woe betide anyone who lets the sail slip into the water.

∧ Sometimes things don't go too well. A few difficult moments are shown here – a catastrophic collision (top), a less serious encounter (left), a trawling spinnaker that stops the boat in its tracks (centre), and a luff that went badly wrong (right), the yachting equivalent of leaving the track in motor racing. It is even possible to combine a luff that ends in a collision with a spinnaker in the water into the bargain, a situation that takes a little longer to resolve…

 **37** Racing is both a leisure activity and a sport played out in an environment that can become hostile and is not without its dangers. Here, a female crew member lost overboard during the Spi Ouest-France regatta is rescued with nothing more serious than a fright for the crew.

 **39** Maxi yachts, seen here racing off the Costa Smeralda (Sardinia), are the most beautiful and spectacular racing yachts ever conceived by man. The hull displaces 30 tons of water as it cleaves through the waves and the bow can reduce the stern of the boat in front to pulp. A cool head and a steady hand are essential at the helm, which is usually entrusted to champions who have already proved themselves at Olympic level and at the helm of large yachts. These monsters are in fact less easy to 'read' and much slower to respond, and demand anticipation and real team work on the part of the crew – a far cry from the instant responses required when sailing a dinghy. Under these conditions, and given the distance, the noise of the wind, waves and winches, and the flapping of the sails, the forward crew cannot even hear orders from the helm.

 **41** Changing the jib on board the maxi yacht *Morning Glory* at Porto Cervo in 1998. The forward crew simply cannot rely on sheer muscle power, given the massive tensions and sheer size of the sail they are handling. They need to use their brains as well as their brawn, and must always be one step ahead, ready for anything and able to deal with last-minute decisions – and even counter-commands from the stern – resulting from the constant changes in wind and tactics. They have to act quickly since, once it's on the deck, a lowered sail is extremely bulky. Also, helmsmen don't like a lot of movement and weight in the forward part of the yacht as this increases pitching and reduces speed.

 43 A regatta is one thing, reliving it in port, glass in hand, is quite another. With faces seamed by the sun and hair still dishevelled by the wind, this is also the time when the crews wait for the results while tidying their yacht and folding the sails before swabbing the deck. For the unlucky, there is also equipment to repair and claims to discuss. When the weather is fine and the light soft, as here at Les Voiles de St Tropez, the process can take hours. In colder climates, yacht-club bars come under siege.

45 Up in the rigging of the maxi yacht *Matador* during a training run off St Thomas (U.S. Virgin Islands). The forward crew are often sent up into the rigging to adjust the mast or work on the halyards used for hoisting the sails. They wear a harness round their waist that also enables them to move about at the end of the boom when changing the spinnaker. There's nothing more frightening than a crew member losing footing on the rigging and swinging free in every direction without being able to regain a hold. If this happens, there's only one solution – to hoist him or her to the top of the mast so as to limit the pendulum effect and the extent of the damage.

The passion for racing

Compulsory sitting-out for the 25 crew members of a maxi yacht (left), with the occasional exception for the owner's friends and family (right).

Mediterranean ports of call

It is hardly surprising that the Mediterranean is the favourite sea of those who were born there and live on its shores. You only have to think of the colour of its waters, its mild climate, its varied cultures and rich history to understand why. It is an ideal sea on which to sail and cruise, provided you are prepared to lay to immediately if the strong wind known variously as the *mistral*, *meltem* or *bora*, depending on the country, starts to blow. But it doesn't last long and the waves subside as quickly as they built up, making the sea probably a little too calm for those who love the open sea and the swell of the ocean. But it is precisely the tranquillity of the Mediterranean that enables you to explore every inch of its coastline, to drop anchor in vividly coloured rocky inlets washed by its deep-blue waters or lay to in quiet, secluded corners. And since there are no tides to worry about, one can sleep soundly at night. Light seems to spill from all around, sometimes to excess when storms are unleashed from summer skies. Then there are the scents and aromas – of pine forests, scrub and olive groves scorched by the sun – and the flavours of local cuisine from Italy, Spain, Catalonia, Provence and North Africa. There is an infinite number of anchorages to choose from and an endless list of destinations. Ports of call, each more alluring than the last, are there for the taking, depending on the direction of the wind and the mood of the moment. Welcome to the Mediterranean.

For many sailors who have travelled throughout the world, Corsica remains one of the most beautiful cruise destinations.
Exploring Marine d'Elbo, on the west coast of Corsica, at the foot of the Scandola Nature Reserve (opposite).
At anchor in the Cala di Volpe, on the Costa Smeralda in northeastern Sardinia (above).

Mediterranean ports of call

A Mediterranean port of call that could be in the Balearic Islands, Greece or Turkey … But this cruising catamaran has dropped anchor

deep in the spectacular inlet of En-Vau, close to the little Provençal
port of Cassis, near Marseilles.

Mediterranean ports of call

As if in a dream, a Carrera glides noiselessly over the calm waters of the Strait of Bonifacio, below the spectacular cliffs of Capo Pertusato. In the distance is the cliff-top village of Bonifacio.

The yacht is helmed by Luca Bassani, the mastermind of the famous Wally Yachts which are to cruiser racing what Ferrari and Maserati are to car racing.

Mediterranean ports of call

Some of the world's most beautiful yachts can be seen in the Mediterranean, especially in the triangle between the Balearic Islands, Sardinia and the Côte d'Azur. The Tiketitoo seen here sailing off Porto Cervo is built entirely of carbon-fibre. She has a canting keel

and four 'stabilizers' designed to give her greater on-course stability. The carbon-fibre sails are unfurled and adjusted by means of a push-button hydraulic system. The anchor is operated in the same way.

The America's Cup

The America's Cup makes people go crazy. At least that's the conclusion you are forced to draw when given the opportunity to follow and experience from the 'inside' the day-to-day progress of several editions of this prestigious event.

How else to explain why sensible and practical captains of industry, who have spent the greater part of their lives building industrial empires by being economical, rational, rigorous and sensible, can spend such colossal amounts of money in a bid to win an – albeit silver – ewer with the singular feature of having no bottom? Added to which, if they succeed in winning it, they are obliged to put it back into play, which means investing even more money, time and effort to try and hold onto it in the face of challenges from the rest of the world. It's totally crazy, especially since the undertaking is almost doomed to failure, given its extraordinary complexity.

In fact, it appears to be these accumulated difficulties that attract the men and women who have decided to spend part of their life, time or money in trying to win the legendary trophy. Famous skippers, humble crew members, designers, technicians, sponsors and financiers are all struck with this America's Cup fever which makes them oblivious to everything else, puts time on hold, galvanizes them with tenfold energy, makes them forget the rest of the world, fosters the most unexpected alliances, provokes the fiercest disagreements, forces those involved to aspire to excellence and gives rise to a series of amazing and unpredictable events. It is way beyond the scope of any ordinary yacht race.

It is thanks to the America's Cup that sailing technology has advanced over the years, that crews have developed new techniques and improved their skills. On land, it's a real circus. Entire ports are reconstructed to accommodate the world's finest racing yachts and their flotilla of accompanying boats, with huge sail-lofts whose security is on a par with that of Fort Knox. All this in an atmosphere tinged with paranoia and mixed with a good dose of acute 'espionage'.

The only rule is that the unimaginable is very likely to happen, the only certainty that nothing is ever certain or definite, and nothing can be taken for granted. Above all, don't take any notice of the official versions, it's what is *not* said that is important. It's certainly a strange world, with its rules and regulations, its clowns, its heroes, its traditions and, above all, its history that is continually re-enacted when, on the day of the final, the challenger, selected during the elimination series, the Louis Vuitton Cup, faces the defending champion. On that day, everything changes and becomes clear. It all becomes simpler and more spectacular, while the exploits of those who have taken part in former Cup challenges surge from history and the memory of famous yachts, classic skippers, revered designers, legendary yacht owners and historic yacht clubs weighs a little more heavily on the minds and shoulders of those who aspire to succeed them and to reach the moment when they can hold the coveted America's Cup and raise it aloft on the evening of their victory.

< To hold the America's Cup and raise it aloft as a symbol of victory has been the dream of all those who, since 1851, have thrown themselves heart and soul into winning the famous silver ewer. The names of those who have enjoyed this privilege are engraved on the base of the bottomless pitcher.

57 This photograph, taken at the time when the U.S. was still undefeated in the America's Cup, shows the 40-foot (12-metre) JIs emerging slowly from the mists of Newport on their way back from a training session off Brenton Tower. The French team suffered under these conditions since Baron Bich's yacht lost a selection race because it missed the buoy – in spite of the fact that the navigator was a certain Éric Tabarly! However, in 1983, *Australia* II didn't have to take advantage of the mist to launch its victorious challenge. Its winged keel was a much more effective weapon.

59 Following the Australian victory in 1983, which put an end to 32 years of U.S. domination, the majestic 40-foot (12-metre) JIs raced in the strong winds that blew off Fremantle in the Indian Ocean. The America's Cup took advantage of the change of venue to become even bigger and more colourful, with twelve challengers hard on the heels of the Australians. Skippered by Marc Pajot, *French Kiss* was in the front line of the battle to introduce commercial sponsorship to the Cup and played a key role in heightening French interest in the competition. All the race photographers have vivid memories of this 1987 edition in Australia and of the 25-knot winds that blew each day, fuelling the spectacular combat beneath the blazing sun, between these powerful heavyweights that sat low in the water. Five months' worth of sailing photos in this vast open-air studio! The images captured at the time are still widely used, all the more so because the competing yachts had not yet been transformed into publicity hoardings.

61 An enduring image of the America's Cup, when defender and challenger pass within a hair's breadth of each other during their unrelenting duel. This was one of the rare moments in the 1987 final when Dennis Conner's *Stars and Stripes* had to pass behind the *Kookaburra* of Ian Murray and Peter Gilmour. The race in which Dennis Conner won back the Cup, four year after his crushing defeat in 1983, makes for one of the most exciting chapters in the amazing history of this competition.

63 By trawling through the regulations in 1988, the New Zealand team led by financier Sir Michael Fay succeeded in launching a challenge against the Americans in a boat of their choice – a huge monohull yacht, the like of which had never been seen before, named *New Zealand* with great pomp and ceremony in Auckland. The American title-holders took up the gauntlet and, after a fierce legal battle, the Kiwis found themselves competing against a catamaran with a devastatingly effective fixed wing, skippered by Dennis Conner, which ran rings round them during their encounter in September 1988. It was subsequently decided to revert to boats that were more evenly matched, and the International America's Cup Class yachts, the Class Americas, were introduced.

65 Circling is a classic manoeuvre that precedes the start of the America's Cup. Each competitor tries to gain the advantage by achieving a more favourable position on the start line. Whereas the 40-foot (12-metre) JIs were sluggish in this type of manoeuvre and tended to lose speed, the Class Americas proved to be much more forward-going and efficient at accelerating. This photograph shows the very first circling manoeuvre of the Class Americas during a training session at Sète in July 1991, between Marc Pajot's F1 and *Il Moro di Venezia*, skippered by Paul Cayard. As you can see, the two skippers lost no time in 'putting the helm hard over'.

Two heroes of the America's Cup: John Bertrand (left), who won in 1983 at the helm of *Australia* II, and his unlucky challenger, Dennis Conner (right), the only yachtsman to have won the Cup four times, in 1974, 1980, 1987 and 1988.

∧ At San Diego, in 1995, the America's Cup adds a new set of incidents to its already colourful history: a huge aircraft carrier crosses the course in the mist (above); a yacht, *Australia One*, breaks her back in the middle of a race, going straight down as the crew jump into the sea (left); returning from the race against the magnificent backdrop of a Californian sunset (right).

∧ In addition to all the technology, the America's Cup requires high levels of organization, a great deal of hard work – which often continues late into the evening (top and left) – and massive resources, for example air-lifting hulls (*Ville de Paris*, centre) in order to save time. Paul Cayard was able to win the Louis Vuitton Cup in 1992 (right) thanks to Italian magnate Raoul Gardini (seen smiling next to the victorious Cayard), one of many to invest colossal sums of money in the event.

71 The two main characteristics of the San Diego course, the venue for the 1988, 1992 and 1995 editions of the America's Cup, were the lack of wind and the size of the swell that comes from the depths of the Pacific – not forgetting the occasional migrating whales that enliven this rather over-tranquil seascape. Although the designers made skilful allowance for these two main factors, the development of the early Class Americas was primarily based on a fairly simple principle – the narrower the yachts, the faster they went!

69 It took time for crews to learn to handle the huge spinnakers of the Class Americas. All the more so because, in 1992, the section of the course raced with fair-wind trims was designed in the form of a Z, requiring several changes of jib. Subsequently, in an attempt to limit the amount of money spent on sails as well as time spent on research and the interminable testing that went with it, America's Cup challengers opted for courses that ran up- and downwind. Although these are certainly more interesting in terms of tactics, they are often much less spectacular to watch.

73 The exclusive domination enjoyed by Team New Zealand in the face of fierce opposition made 1995 one of the most remarkable editions in the history of the America's Cup. The team won 41 of their 42 races, only losing on the day that the late lamented Sir Peter Blake, the formidable driving force of the challenge, did not sail on *New Zealand*, better known as *Black Magic*. This gave rise to the legend of his favourite lucky red socks that became the symbol of the Kiwi victory.

75 *Nippon* and *France* 2-3 during a training session off San Diego in 1995. The sight of a Class America bearing down on you, manned by a crew shouting its right of way as its bow bursts through the waves in a shower of spray, is an unnerving experience for most ordinary mortals. For the helmsmen who steer these 25-ton monsters to within a millimetre, there is no margin for error. The forward crew member perched on the bow is indicating the relative position of the two yachts and checking the countdown. In the foreground, the crew member trimming the jib controls the power required by the helmsman – he has several tons of tension at his fingertips.

After winning in 1992 on board the *America* 3, American billionaire Bill Koch tried out an all-female crew (left). This didn't worry Sir Peter Blake (right), the driving force of the crushing New Zealand victory in 1995.

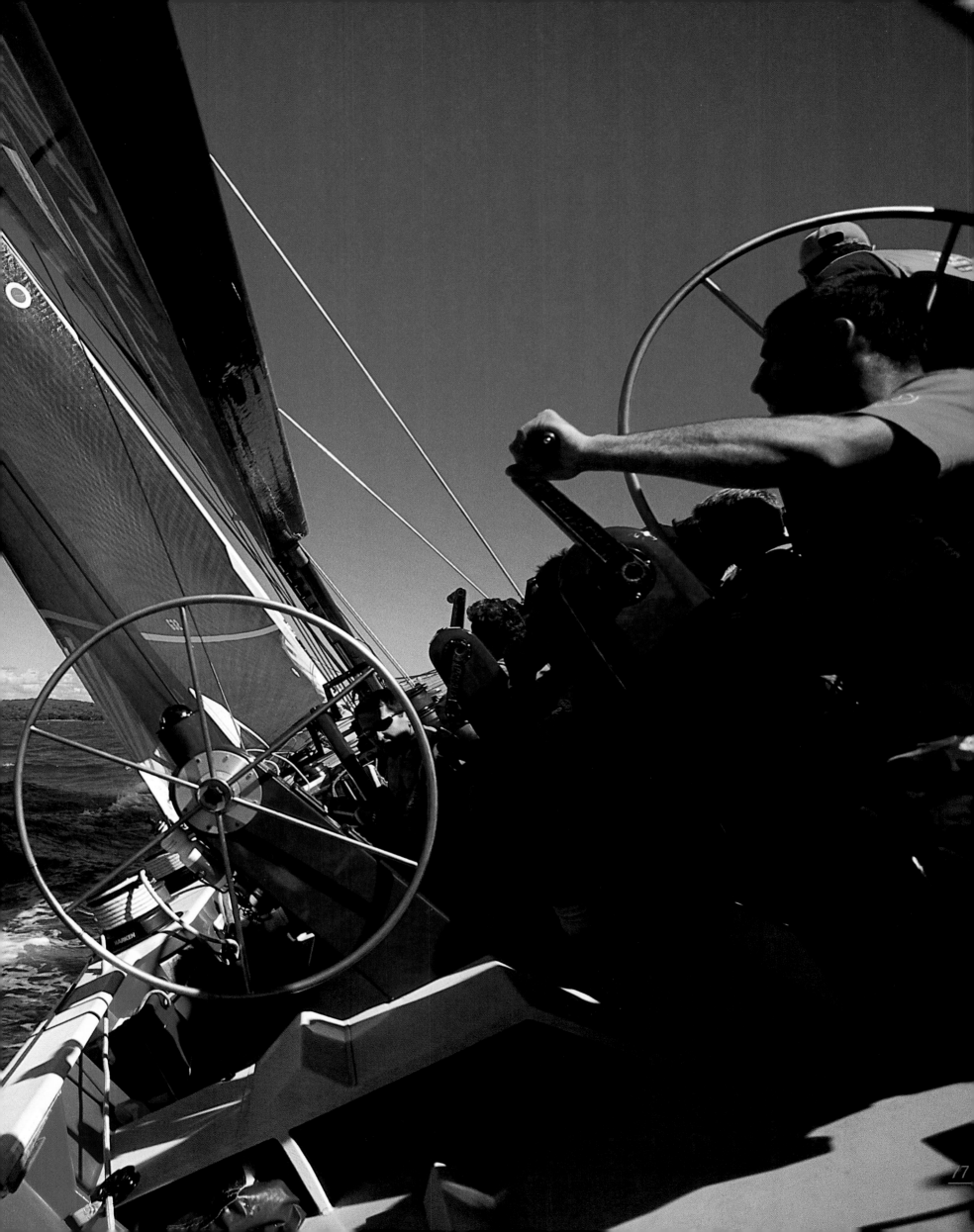

 **77**   The America's Cup 2000 was held in New Zealand. Here, the New York Yacht Club's *Young America* and *6th Sense* helmed by Bertrand Pacé, are sailing close alongside in the Hauraki Gulf. In the distance, in the centre of Auckland bay, is the dormant Rangitoto volcano – which one hopes will stay that way. This course, surrounded by middle-altitude relief, is undoubtedly the most demanding in the Cup's history. It is tactical, varied and complete, with days of fine weather, sea breezes and calm seas or 'back-breaking' swell. The crews love it and it even enables a yacht that is slower but well-manned to gain the upper hand. However, the teams' main objective throughout the interminable preparations for the race is to make sure they have the fastest yacht. With only one or two exceptions in the 32 editions of the America's Cup, the fastest yacht has always won.

79   The great skippers of the America's Cup have demonstrated truly amazing skill at the helm. Here, Paul Cayard, at the helm of *America One* (on the right in the photo) in the final of the Louis Vuitton Cup 2000, completes his turn and passes between *Luna Rossa* and the boat of the race committee whose hearts were in their mouths. This daring manoeuvre was so sudden and instinctive that it even surprised his own crew, who didn't have time to trim the sails!

 **81**   The crews of the Class Americas – here the crew of *Luna Rossa* during the Louis Vuitton Cup 2000 – are so good at their job that they don't notice the spray, the noise, the flapping of the sails or even their opponent. Hundreds of hours' training have made their movements instinctive. As they prepare for the start, the only things that matter are the countdown and the position of their yacht in relation to the start line on which all eyes are fixed. At the helm of *Luna Rossa*, Francesco de Angelis had a free hand for six consecutive years in his bid to be the first skipper to bring the America's Cup back to Europe.

 83   With a following wind and the spinnakers hoisted, the yacht behind has time to blanket the one in front and gradually make up ground. Overtaking is a different matter and an entire race can be fought out sailing in close company. One of the opponents has only to gain two or three yards to change the outcome of the duel. Here, during a decisive race that will take her into the semi-final of the Louis Vuitton Cup 2000, *6th Sense* (top of the photo) will blanket *America One* and then overtake her, thereby maintaining the chance of going into the following round.

The America's Cup

An ambitious hull decoration and a smart, well-concealed keel are two unmistakable elements of the America's Cup in the twenty-first century.

∧ Mishaps in Auckland bay: in spite of its splendidly
decorated hull, Abracadabra loses control of its boom as it
begins to luff (top); 6th Sense collides with Stars and Stripes
(left); Luna Rossa and America One become embroiled in a
demented ballet during the final of the Louis Vuitton Cup
2000, the most spectacular edition since it was inaugurated
in 1983 (centre, right and opposite, left).

∧ *Young America* returns to port with all pumps in action (top). The yacht that was supposed to bring the Cup back to the United States in 2000 broke her back on the waves of the Hauraki Gulf. As the bow of *Luna Rossa* cleaves though the waves (centre), the boom of *6th Sense* (right) hits the water but survives the impact, even though it was never designed to undergo such pressure. The unfathomable mysteries of technology.

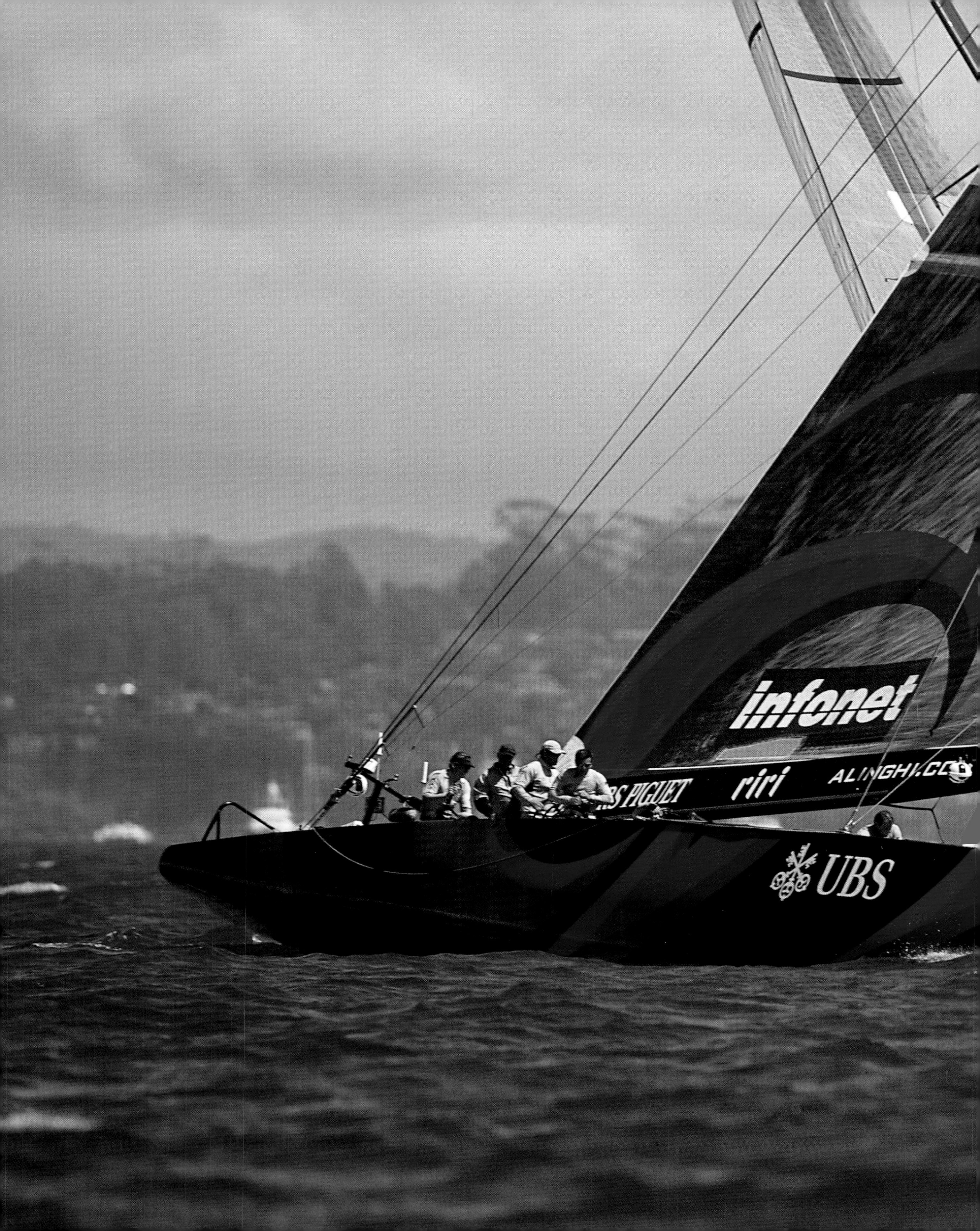
infonet
riri
UBS

89 Three years later, in 2003, the same players met again in Auckland for an action replay with one difference – most of the competitors left in the race seemed to be from New Zealand! Furthermore, Russell Coutts (helm), Brad Butterworth and Murray Jones (tacticians), Warwick Fleury (mainsail) and Simon Dubney (forward sails) were now the challengers and were sailing the red and black *Alinghi*, fitted out by the young Swiss millionaire Ernesto Bertarelli. Once again, they won with a score of 5–0, but this time at the expense of their former teammates of Team New Zealand, skippered by the young Dean Barker. Having abandoned two races due to technical problems, including a spectacular unmasting, the All Blacks of the sailing world could do nothing against the amazing Swiss challenger who took the America's Cup back to Europe for the first time since 1851.

91 By winning the America's Cup for the third consecutive time in 2003, Russell Coutts (seen here celebrating his victory in Auckland, in 2000) joined Charlie Barr and Dennis Conner in the annals of sailing history. He and Conner are the only yachtsmen in the history of the America's Cup to have won as challenger and then as defending champion. However, his fellow New Zealanders still find it hard to forgive him for having taken the Cup away from his own country. Russell Coutts is an exceptional helmsman and skipper, as well as a charismatic leader who, with the backing and support of Ernesto Bertarelli and Team Alinghi, has proved his ability to mount a winning challenge from scratch. In the run-up to the 32nd edition of the America's Cup, to be held in Europe in 2007, Coutts has embarked upon a major program of renovation that should contribute significantly to the competition's reputation as one of the great international sporting events.

87 Contrary to the impression given by this photo, the final of the America's Cup 2000, held for the first time in Auckland, wasn't fiercely contested. Team New Zealand, with Russell Coutts at the helm, was superior in every respect and easily disposed of the Italian challenger, *Luna Rossa*, skippered by Francesco de Angelis, with an unequivocal score of 5–0. For the photographers, who aren't allowed in front of the competitors, this was an unmissable opportunity as, for once, the winner appeared in the foreground. Since it's impossible to get really close, you need a steady hand as you hold up your 600 mm telephoto lens.

The America's Cup

Ernesto Bertarelli (left) will go down in sailing history as the man who brought the America's Cup back to Europe, with wild support from spectators (right) when the yachts hit the shore. *Alinghi* flying before the unmasted *New Zealand* (centre), an image that symbolized the 2003 edition.

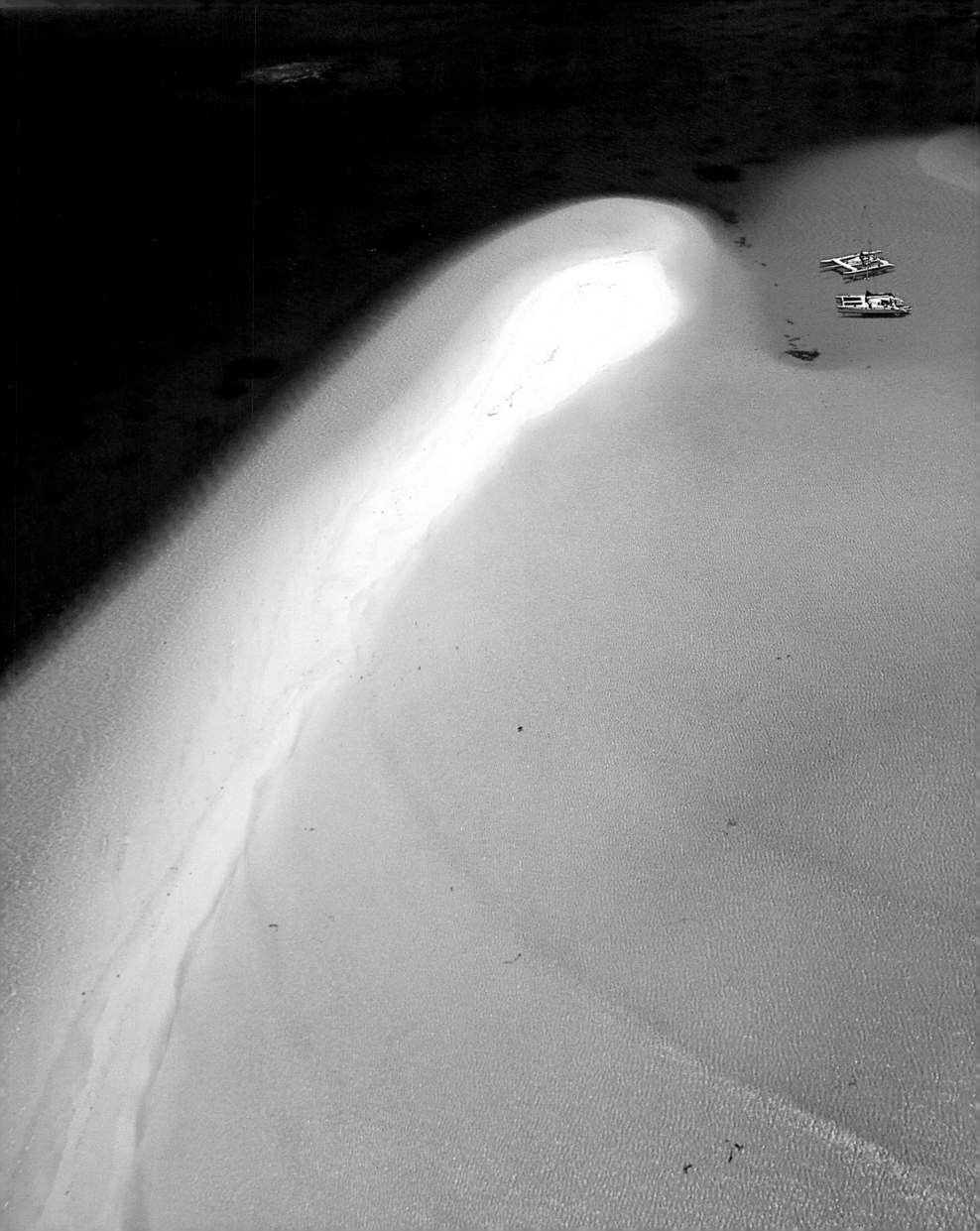

Tropical ports of call

Sailing in the tropics is a breathtaking, magical experience. The moment you enter tropical waters four physical sensations strike you. The first is the gentle touch of the trade winds – warm, dry, steady breezes that caress your skin and give the sea its beautiful contours and magnificent deep-blue colour, highlighted by the occasional glint of a flying fish as it tries to escape a predator. The second is visual, as you come across a channel through a coral reef and discover the unique tropical blue of its lagoon. There's always a gentle shiver of excitement as you approach the Tobago Cayes, Bora-Bora, the Maldives, the Seychelles or New Caledonia, the delicious feeling that you'll soon be dropping anchor, that life will be sweeter and the world more beautiful as the blue of the sea is complemented by the green of the coconut palms in a perfect balance of colour. The third sensation is related to sound – the distant pounding of the waves breaking on a coral reef, a constant background noise that becomes clearer in the evening when the wind stops blowing through the rigging.

The final seductive sensation is linked to taste and experienced as the setting sun sinks behind the clouds, bathing the boats at anchor in its soft, pink light. This is the time of day when the aromas of Creole sausage and acras begin to fill the cockpits, and glasses begin to chink as *ti'punches* are prepared.

Breathtaking, magical, enchanting – unforgettable.

One of the most beautiful anchorages in the world – the lagoon on Nokanhui island, near the Isle of Pines (New Caledonia) in the southwest Pacific. But it's suitable only for catamarans.
Dohnis, the traditional boats of the Maldives, in the Indian Ocean (above).

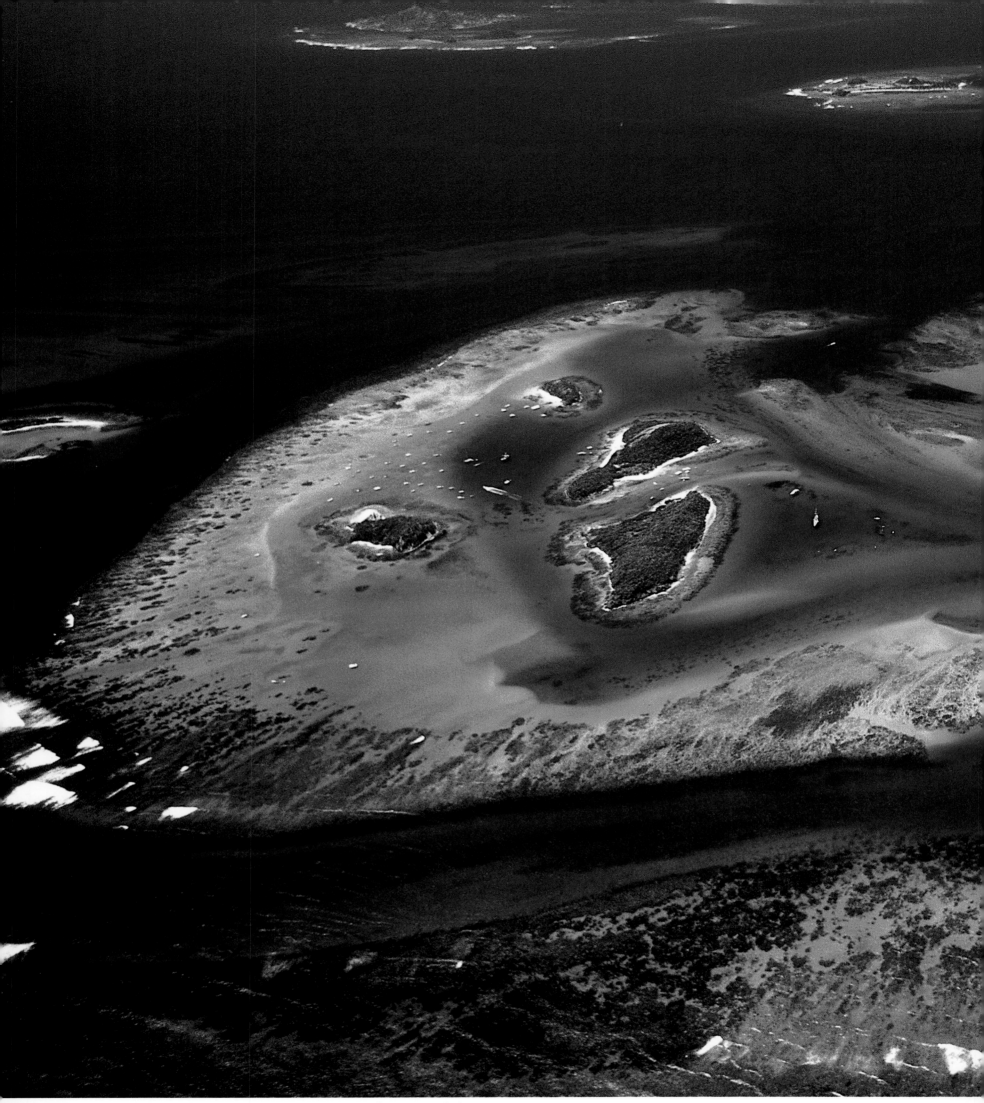

Tropical ports of call

The anchorage of the Tobago Cayes, in the southern Grenadines, is one of the great natural harbours in the West Indies.

You won't be alone but it's hardly surprising, the gentle trade winds
and clear waters are so delightful.

Tropical ports of call

Bora-Bora. Go and see for yourself why this is the most beautiful, most exquisite anchorage in the world. It's all to do with the colour of the water, the idyllic setting, the beaches, the vast numbers of

fish in all shapes and sizes and the situation of the islands. You have the delicious feeling that you could stay here forever and that time simply doesn't have the same meaning as elsewhere. Out of this world.

Sunset in Praslin, in the Seychelles. This is the time to
come and dig in the sand for *tek tek*, small shellfish that

taste delicious when they are fried in a little oil and flavoured
with a touch of garlic and parsley.

Ocean racing

racing

< Conceived by Éric Tabarly and designed by Alain Thébault, *Hydroptère*, a hydrofoil trimaran, seen here sailing at 30 plus knots in the Baie de Quiberon, may well represent the shape of things to come in the field of ocean yacht racing. In the next few decades, crews will have to become increasingly adept at sailing above the water. One heck of a gamble on the future! From a photographic point of view, it's worth wasting a few shots in a bid to capture this amazing image, made possible by a fairly slow shutter speed that recreates the effect of movement that is so difficult to control. You also have to have complete confidence in your pilot since this photo was taken from a helicopter that matched its speed to that of the yacht.

Initially confined to the vicinity of ports and coastal waters, ocean racing was the brainchild of a few rebels who much preferred sailing on the open sea to battling it out with their contemporaries around three buoys. Of course, there were the great classics created by the yacht clubs – Fastnet, Sydney-Hobart, Newport-the Bermudas – before World War Two. But it was yachtsmen like Blondie Hasler (creator of the British transatlantic yacht race), Sir Francis Chichester (the first man to sail single-handed around the world), Éric Tabarly, Peter Blake and Philippe Jeantot who made ocean racing what it is today.

The courage, vision and determination of these men showed the younger generation that the world's oceans could be much more than a nautical playing field, that they are also a place of extraordinary adventure, an environment in which nothing can be achieved without respect for nature and an element of danger. The long list of sailors and yachtsmen lost at sea is a stark reminder.

Under the pressure of competition, yachts are being continually modified and improved, and records broken. With their pivoting or canting keels and streamlined rigging, monohull ocean-racing yachts have become larger, faster, more powerful and more technically advanced. However, when it comes to ocean crossings, the multihull yachts based on the design of Polynesian canoes are the ultimate weapons. Structural and technical advances mean that they can now cross the Atlantic in under five days and it won't be long before they are sailing round the world in less than fifty. The trimarans used in ocean racing are the fastest yachts in the world, in any category. They sail into the wind at a speed of 17 knots, i.e. 50 percent faster than a yacht in the America's Cup. The yachts of the future (represented by the racing hydrofoil, opposite) are already sailing partially out of the water and promise to produce even more astounding performances. However, it's the individuals and their achievements that stick in people's minds – Éric Tabarly who won the 1976 transatlantic race at the helm of his maxi yacht designed for a crew of 15, Yves Parlier who rebuilt his mast in an isolated mooring in some far-flung corner of the world and Ellen MacArthur who, at the age of 25, held her own against the best yachtsmen in the Vendée Globe. One thing is certain: ocean racing is a sport that will continue to fire the public imagination.

105 Like Christophe Auguin, seen here 'planing' in *Geodis*, those yachtsmen who sail single-handed around the world in the Vendée Globe know how to pick up speed under the right weather conditions. Their 60-foot (18-metre) monohull yachts are designed – as is *Geodis* by Finot and Conq – to pick up speed in a fair wind. Sailing into the wind is a completely different matter, and a great deal less comfortable, since the yachts' flat hulls hit the waves with unexpected force.

103 Crews have gradually learned to make single-hull maxi yachts ride the waves like ordinary sailing dinghies when wind and sea are strong enough, as here, in Marc Pajot's attempt on the Mediterranean record. However, this surfing session was short lived since the boom holding the spinnaker out over the bow didn't stand the strain. Designed by Swiss yachtsman Pierre Fehlmann, yachts of the Grand Mistral class were intended to become the largest monotype ocean-racers, but the project was ultimately shelved, probably because it was ahead of its time.

107 A spectacular swell and the light of the open sea on the ketch rigging of Alain Gautier's *Bagages Supérior*, winner of the Vendée Globe 1992. Although this photograph could have been taken in the Roaring Forties, where the light is apparently just as amazing, it was in fact taken a few days after the start, off Les Sables-d'Olonne, in a typical sea after an Atlantic gale.

109 Although the problems of calm weather have been greatly reduced with the development of ocean racing, skippers still fear it as much as storms. Anticyclones are responsible for the greatest time differences since some yachts are able to take advantage of the wind better than others. With advances in weather-forecasting techniques and on-board communications systems making it possible to find information on the Internet, ocean-racing skippers have gradually become weather experts in their own right and are now able to manage their strategy without the help of outside planners.

Ocean racing

Left to right: Christophe Auguin, Alain Gautier and Michel Desjoyeaux, three great winners of the Vendée Globe, the ultimate race devised and organized by Philippe Jeannot.

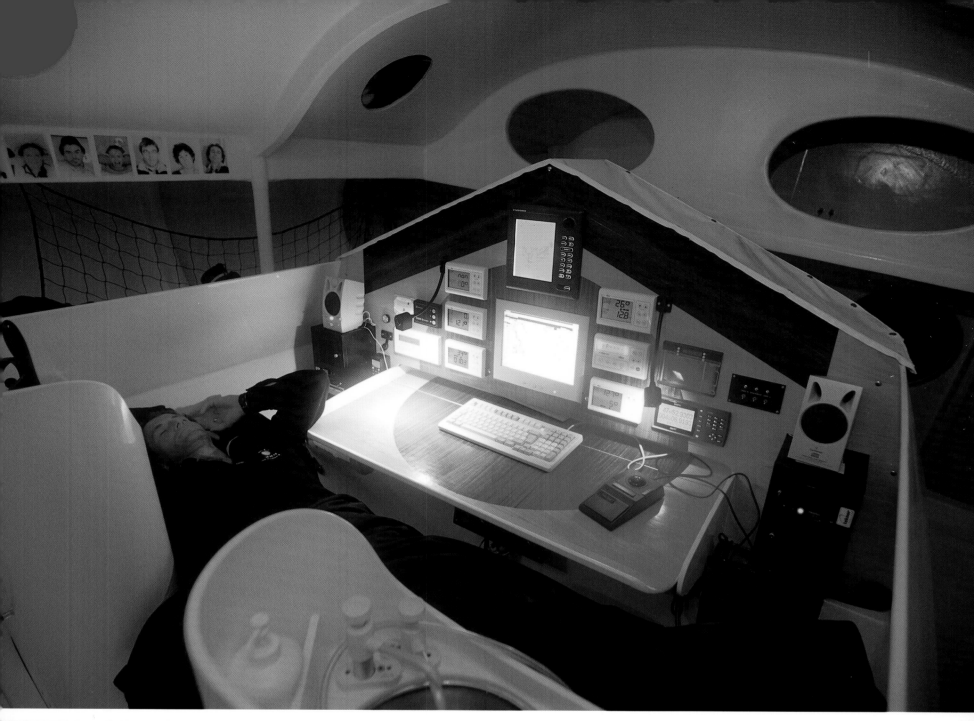

< Coming into port after sailing single-handed around the world is an extremely emotional experience. After spending 100 days alone at sea, far from the daily round of people and events, these yachtsmen and women are suddenly faced with an enthusiastic welcome from an ecstatic crowd, like the one received by Ellen MacArthur when she came second in the Vendée Globe 2000. These are moments of sheer joy for everyone concerned. And rightly so, since the general public has shared the anxieties and emotions of these long-distance sailors throughout their journey. The start of the Vendée Globe is all the more emotional because the dangers of this type of racing are very real.

∧ Alone at sea – where sleeping, eating, day-to-day maintenance, navigating, communicating, making adjustments and steering are all part of the daily routine of ocean racing – individual yachtsmen and women create interiors adapted to their own particular style of sailing and way of life. Michel Desjoyeaux (top) even designed a living space on a pivot mechanism so as to maintain the feeling of being horizontal when the yacht was listing.

 **113** Jean-Luc Nélias' *Belgacom* performs a spectacular nose-dive during the Grand Prix de Fécamp 2001 – the bows plunge down into the water while the rudder rises into the air. The helmsman has lost control of the ocean-racing trimaran as the wind continues to blow in the rigging. There are several possible solutions: the crew could relieve the pressure in the sails, the bows (and this would be a real stroke of luck) might re-emerge on their own or the stalemate could continue and the yacht capsize. One minor detail – there's a man in the huge wave on the left, face down on the netting.

 **117** Bottleneck at the starting buoy in the Jacques Vabre 2001 transatlantic race. The multihull ocean racers, developed mainly in France, are incontestably the fastest yachts in the world. Although not yet widely known outside France, these are undoubtedly the yachts of the future. Their championship comprises two major ocean races and three or four Grand Prix depending on the year.

 **115** Alain Gautier's *Foncia* 2 has reared up and is sailing entirely on her port hydrofoil and the back end of the float as she bears down on the *Bonduelle* helmed by Jean Le Cam which, although she appears stationary, is in fact sailing at a speed of 25 plus knots. When this photo was taken, the *Foncia* 2 was sailing in her first Grand Prix (Lorient 2002) and had not been quite perfected. The hydrofoil was stuck in the lowest position (where it gives the most power) and the mechanism that controls the sheet of the mainsail, which usually makes it possible to release excess power in the sails, was jammed in the central position. It would hardly be overstating it to say that *Foncia* 2 was not entirely under control.

 **119** Sailing close alongside at 25 knots for hours on end remains the prerogative of the crews of the multihull yachts that cover stupendous distances during each day's sailing. This type of sailing pushes crew and equipment to the limit, but gives a sensation of speed and weightlessness unique to this type of yacht.

 121 Whether sailing single- or double-handed, the forecastle of a trimaran is not very broad and the movements of modern multihulls are extremely abrupt, especially when sailing against the waves. Good sea legs are essential. Skippers prefer to race double-handed (although this doesn't preclude accidents) because they don't have to think twice before pushing their yacht to the limit and, more importantly, because a single-handed race on this type of extremely and even over-sensitive craft increasingly resembles a game of Russian roulette.

Ocean racing

Laurent Bourgnon and Florence Arthaud, two skippers who made their mark on the history of the Route du Rhum, the famous transatlantic race created by Michel Etévenon.

∧ The trimaran F*ujifilm* off the southwest tip of Ushant Island, in a counter-current wind, during the Course des Phares 2002. The sea is not always beautiful and sometimes looks more like a chaotic expanse of bumps and hollows, especially when the current is running counter to the direction of the waves, creating a spectacular, seething mass of water. Fortunately, the distance covered by *Fuji* on this particular outing was relatively short. With a wind of just under 20 knots and a swell of between 6½ and 10 feet (2–3 metres) running against a current with a coefficient of 99, weather conditions weren't particularly bad. In winter, when the swell is between 20 and 26 feet (6–8 metres), the wind force 9 and the current has a coefficient of 100, it's best not linger in this formidable stretch of water which, over the years, has become known as the 'Trou du Diable' ('devil's cauldron').

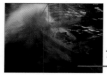

125 The main characteristic of multihull ocean-racing yachts is that they are extremely fast and tend to get drenched by spray, as demonstrated here by *Commodore Explorer* during a bid to break the Mediterranean record. By sailing this catamaran non-stop around the world in under 80 days, in 1993, Bruno Peyron and his crew of four wrote another chapter in the history of sailing. A few years later, their exploit not only gave rise to The Race but also to a new generation of giant catamarans.

127 *Playstation* leaving the Needles near the Isle of Wight, off the south coast of England. This is another good spot for spectacular sailing since the wind usually blows against the current as it flows out of the Solent, speeding up the progress of yachts negotiating the sand banks scattered throughout this stretch of water. *PlayStation*, designed by the Morelli–Melvin team, financed and skippered by American billionaire Steve Fossett, is the largest racing catamaran in the world, and has successively smashed all records she has attempted. In particular, in the spring of 2001 she achieved a spectacular transatlantic crossing in the record time of 4 days, 17 hours, 28 minutes and 6 seconds. Sailing against the sea, she does however have a tendency to pitch and, although her bows have been extended and raised, this doesn't appear to have had much effect.

129 *Club Med*, another giant that eats up the miles, broke most speed records when she won the first edition of The Race in 2001. Photographed here in a strong swell off Barcelona, the starting point of this 'no-limits', non-stop, round-the-world race, the catamaran designed and built by Gilles Ollier and skippered by Grant Dalton outclassed her two 'sister ships', *Team Adventure* (Cam Lewis) and *Innovation Explorer* (Loïck Peyron).

131 Victory parade for the winners of The Race in Marseilles. You usually see only photos of the winner at the finish of the major yacht races, but what goes on in the flotilla of spectators' boats following on behind is just as interesting. An armada, in which large speedboats and motor-yachts vie for position with all kinds of inflatables and small boats under varying degrees of control, creates waves that form chaotic and sometimes heavy seas. If you're participating, the spectacle is positively Dantesque and it's even worse at night since no one has any lights and everyone is travelling at full speed to keep up with the multihulls. Scary!

133 For the 15-strong crew, life on board a giant catamaran is not the most uncomfortable experience in the world since there is space in both hulls. Under wet conditions, the hull can even offer shelter from the spray while the crew is on watch. But then there are the movements of the boat, which are as sudden for those on watch as for those trying to sleep inside.

Ocean racing

The Race: the victorious arrival of *Club Med* in Marseilles in March 2001 was cause for great celebration.

∧ By winning back the Jules Verne Trophy on board *Orange* in 2002, Bruno Peyron and his crew demonstrated that it was now possible to sail round the world in under 50 days – and there's no shortage of candidates bidding to break this record. Skippers must be able to delegate while keeping their eye on everything – navigation in the charthouse, steering a course at night, trimming the sails, the condition of the crew and the state of their equipment.

⋀ Whether you're moving about on the netting by day or at night, even in rough seas, or sailing through the dawn at high speed, life on board a big multihull racing yacht like *Orange* is punctuated by constant changes of sail that demand a great deal of care and organization, in view of the massive effort involved.

Atlantic ports of call

The sea is greener, the air cooler and the landscape animated by the movement of tides. Clouds filter the light and there's always a passing trawler or cargo ship and a swell that seems to come from nowhere. It's windy, exhilarating and constantly changing. This is the Atlantic or rather its offshoot, the English Channel – a region of depressions, warm fronts and heavy skies, anchorages and little ports pervaded by Celtic, Norman or Gaelic influence. There are great sailors in this part of the world, and they respect their boats – they know how to get the best out of them, tacking beautifully and enjoying the counter-currents under the watchful eye of the lighthouses. Here, more than anywhere else in the world, people respect those who earn their living at sea – in the fishing industry, the navy and the merchant navy. Even those who live and work ashore have learnt to come to terms with the bad weather that blows in from the sea, by building single-storey houses sheltered from the strong westerly winds.

The islands of Sein, Ushant and Scilly are like huge vessels that endure more storms than most, while the lighthouses of Fastnet, Land's End and La Jument stand like sentinels in the vastness of the Atlantic, pounded by the waves and shrouded in stories and legends. It wasn't around these solitary outposts that the joys of sailing were discovered, but rather in the more sheltered waters of ports like Cowes, Le Havre, La Rochelle and Trinité-sur-Mer. To experience the charms of the Atlantic to the full, head for Scotland, Ireland or the secluded shores of the more distant islands of Madeira and the Azores.

With its dozens of enchanted islands, secluded inlets and treacherous currents, the Morbihan Gulf is one of the most magical stretches of water in the whole of Brittany, where there is no shortage of delightful ports of call.
A formation of seaweed (above).

Atlantic ports of call

Belle-Île-en-Mer embodies the irresistible charm of an Atlantic island set in the
ocean. On the west side of the island, the anchorage of Sterr Wen at the foot of

the Poulains lighthouse can only be reached in calm weather. Its secluded inlets are
not unlike those of Ireland and Scotland.

Atlantic ports of call

Yachting was born of the Atlantic where it developed more rapidly and intensely than anywhere else in the world. The Atlantic also gave birth to the America's Cup, the Admiral's Cup and the Fastnet Cup.

The Solent, the channel separating England (left) from the Isle of Wight (right), remains one of the Meccas of the sailing world and each year welcomes thousands of yachts of all ages, sizes and classes.

The spirit of sailing

It all began without warning, one fine autumn day, on the quayside in St Tropez. It must have been in 1989 and it was probably a Tuesday because, in the Nioulargue, the yachts traditionally begin racing on Wednesday. On that particular day, for the first time, yachts like *Orion*, *Shenandoah*, *Altair*, *Puritan* and *Lelantina* were moored side by side in the tiny port, offering a truly breathtaking spectacle of beauty and majesty. The revival of classic sailing had begun. In the past, the Nioulargue had been a fairly low-key event for more or less modern racing yachts. Suddenly, when people saw the majestic rigging, brass outfittings and teak decks of these old yachts, hitherto just part of the family, they experienced a huge surge in popularity.

It was *Altair* that really started it all, since her companions were still more or less well-maintained family yachts. Completely restored with an unprecedented attention to authenticity and detail, this huge schooner with her fore-and-aft rigging was a spectacle in her own right. There was one unbelievable moment when, on the media boat carrying photographers from all over the world, the clicking of the cameras gradually subsided as they were returned to their cases. The photographers simply wanted to experience the immense pleasure of watching the yacht under sail, staring in open-eyed wonder like kids, awed by the beauty of her lines, her graceful rigging, immaculate sails, the elegance of her crew in their white overalls, and the speed of the carefully orchestrated manoeuvres executed in complete silence. It was a truly unforgettable experience!

The same thing happened two years later when *Tuiga* joined the event. Then came *Kentra*, *Moonbeam*, *Cintra* and the huge *Adix*. Gradually, yacht owners all over Europe began to search out old yachts in varying states of disrepair, small, large, famous or just battered old hulks. Small fortunes and any amount of time and ingenuity were spent in restoring them, with great attention paid to authenticity and quality of detail. On the water, what had been a simple parade became a spectacle of amazing beauty when the classic yachts began to compete. In the early stages, it was a fairly amateurish affair and there were times when you could hear the VHF radios of the skippers – who hadn't quite got the hang of this kind of sport – asking the race officials which way they should cross the start line! Gradually, the crews began to make greater demands on the majestic rigging of these floating museum pieces, offering an extraordinary spectacle the like of which only a few of our grandfathers had been privileged to witness.

In the wake of the Nioulargue, which subsequently became the Voiles de St Tropez and has remained the high point of the season, other classic yacht races were organized – Sardinia, Imperia on the Riviera dei Fiori, the Régates Royales (Cannes) and Monaco Classic Week, which also welcomes old motorboats and motor-yachts. In the Atlantic, the big yachting events – Brest, Douarnenez and Rouen – also celebrate renewed public interest in this maritime heritage.

< There are magical moments at sea and in the sky. The huge, white geneker of the three-masted *Creole*, here sailing off Saint-Tropez during the Nioulargue 1991, is about to be lowered. A crew member stands ready at the end of the bow, but his troubles are only just beginning. In a few seconds, the halyard will snap and the huge sail will fall into the water.

 **145** Fore-and-aft riggings, with their characteristic gaffsail surmounted by a gaff-topsail, are the most elegant and beautiful of the classic-yacht riggings. When three such fine examples as *The Lady Anne* (Fife, 1912), *Tuiga* (Fife, 1909) and *Mariette* (Herreshoff, 1915) sail close alongside in the Solent, it's as if you've stepped back in time to the early twentieth century, when these magnificent sailing ships were the fastest in the world. Frank Beken of Cowes was first in a line of great marine photographers to immortalize these scenes. He would take up his position in a small boat in the middle of the Solent, holding the camera at arm's length in both hands, the shutter being fired by biting on a rubber ball gripped in his teeth! Nowadays, things are a bit easier.

 **147** The 40-foot (12-metre) JIs, with their fore-and-aft rigging, are relatively few and far between, and *Cintra* (Fife, 1909) is probably the only one still seaworthy. Here she is making the classic tack that brings contestants to the finish of what used to be the Niolargue. In the background is the old district of La Ponche, dominated by the red-and-yellow tower of the church of St Tropez. This venue is an absolute must for lovers of classic yachts.

 **149** The *Orion* (Nicholson, 1910), a huge schooner with fore-and-aft sails, was one of the forerunners of the classic yacht revival of the 1980s and 1990s. Here she is under shortened sail at the entrance to the Gulf of St Tropez. In the distance, the Estérel Massif is bathed in the characteristic light of a Provençal autumn, when the sea breezes become a rather cool 'westerly'.

 151 Although it is impossible not to admire the elegance of a big schooner like *Altair* (Fife, 1931), another great name in the classic yacht revival, you may prefer a cheeky little dinghy like *Billie Jane*. This charming encounter took place on a beautiful day during the Nioulargue. The image is well known, being recorded simultaneously by some forty international photographers all crammed into the same boat.

The spirit of sailing

New sails and carefully coiled rigging – the classic yachts are lavished with care by their owners, both at sea and in port.

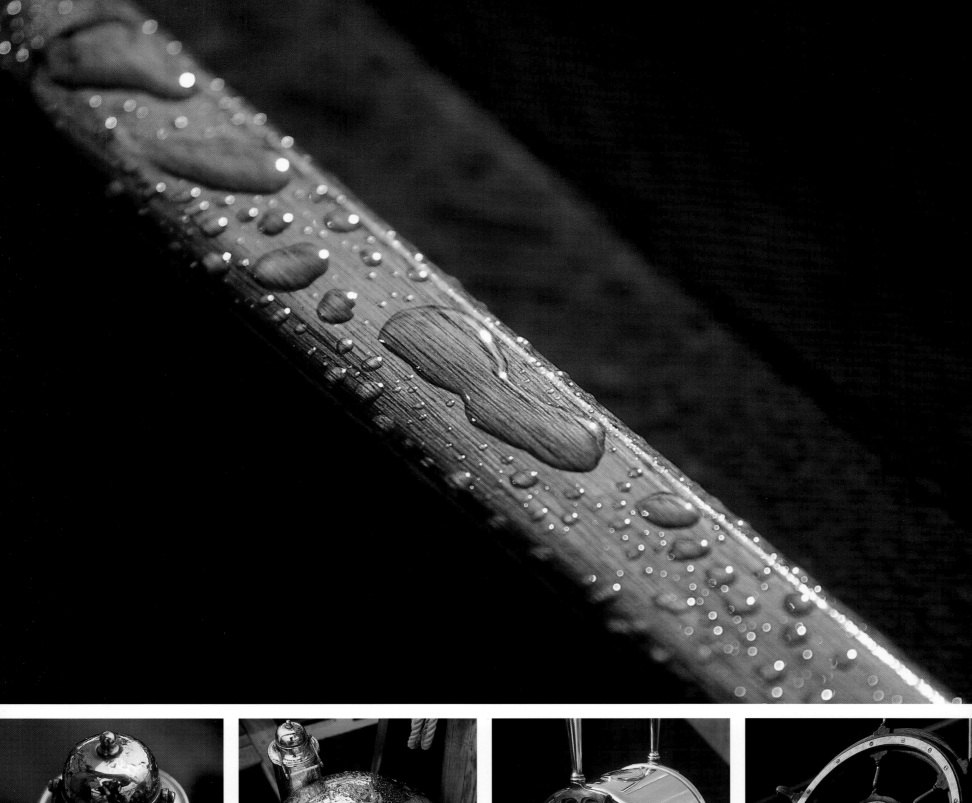

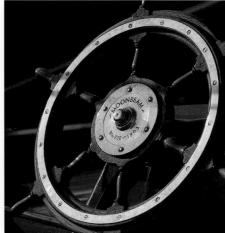

∧ With their natural-coloured sails reminiscent of the canvas used in the past, immaculately varnished wood that is continually refurbished, and brass outfittings and navigational equipment polished daily, the classic yachts have been restored to the highest degree of authenticity.

157 The more sails a yacht has, the lower the freeboard, the finer the hull and the greater the elegance. On board *Tuiga*, which has a tendency to list, the passing water is never very far from the deck and sometimes takes the crew by surprise. In a fair wind on a calm sea, one can try hanging a camera over the side just above the surface of the water since in such conditions the yacht cleaves a fairly regular furrow through the waves. At least, under normal conditions – in some circumstances it could be playing with fire.

155 Gradually, the magnificently restored, single-hull yachts that once paraded at a slow, dignified pace began to race sedately. Then their crews began to make greater demands on their majestic riggings, until they were sailing in winds and at speeds not really suitable for this type of craft. It's a very long time since the J Class *Candida* (Nicholson, 1929) competed in this way. Here she is being pushed to the limit during training by the Corum Sailing Team, despite an unfavourable east wind in the Bay of St Tropez. It is fascinating to see just how much the best modern crews enjoy sailing these historic yachts, and try to emulate the movements of their counterparts of two or three generations ago.

159 As the *mistral* begins to gust, the ketch *Karenita* (Alden, 1929) ploughs through the waves in the Gulf of St Tropez. With the bulwark in the water, the crew have their work cut out. The movements of classic yachts are very stately and gradual but, once they pick up speed, they are not easy to stop. The stronger the wind, the more they list and the lower they sink in the water without building up much speed.

161 Rarely has a yacht been so passionately loved by her owner as *Pen Duick*, with which Éric Tabarly discovered the joys of sailing and the art of tacking. Although he went on to own much faster racing yachts, Tabarly has always had a soft spot for his first *Pen Duick* – he gave the name to ten later yachts – and, as is his wont, has communicated this enduring affection to all those who have seen him sail. It has to be said that, with her heavy fore-and-aft rigging and low freeboard, the little 'coal tit' was quite a handful!

The spirit of sailing

Splice, whipping, sheepshank, palm, bowline and sheet bend – strange terms that form part of the science of running rigging for such masters as Éric Tabarly (right).

∧ When it comes to classic yachts, the interiors are just as good as the exteriors. On deck, modern outfitters have worked hard to recreate bronze parts and winches that are in keeping with the traditional style of these yachts. Even better, some carbon-fibre masts look like wood!

∧ The interior fittings are nearly always in varnished wood that has to be regularly treated in spite of the busy sailing schedules of today's classic yachts. From left to right: gangway on board *Kentra*, wardrooms of *Viola*, *Oiseau de Feu*, decorated with numerous maritime objects, and Tuiga, detail and wardroom of the motor-yacht *Mauna Laua*.

167 As the bulwark of the ketch *Gloria* goes into the water under the force of a squally east wind, the Scottish crew don't seem unduly bothered and make not the slightest attempt to shorten sail. This photo was taken in 1987, at the point where the Gulf of St Tropez opens out into the sea, during one of the editions of the Nioulargue that marked the revival of classic yachts. This was probably the first opportunity to take an aerial photograph of an old yacht under such pressure.

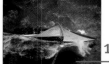

165 The sumptuous J Class *Shamrock* (Nicholson, 1930) was the last and undoubtedly the most prestigious yacht owned by Sir Thomas Lipton. She raced in the 1930s against *Endeavour* (Nicholson, 1934) and *Velsheda* (Nicholson, 1933), two equally magnificent J Class yachts. After having been stripped of their lead ballast during World War II and then abandoned in tidal reservoirs, all three craft underwent positively Herculean labour to restore them to their former glory. They are now in superb condition, and compete together several times a year on the world's most prestigious courses. An encounter between the only seaworthy J Class yachts (*Endeavour*, *Velsheda*, *Shamrock*, *Cambria*, *Astra* and *Candida*) remains, however, a dream for the many aficionados of these legendary yachts. One day, perhaps.

169 An unlikely encounter between a small, unknown yacht and the J Class *Cambria*, magnificently restored in Australia, one of the few boats in this class designed in 1928 by the famous Scottish designer William Fife. The encounter took place in the Solent, during the celebrations held to mark the 150th anniversary of the America's Cup, in August 2001. The occasion brought together the most beautiful yachts and most famous yachtsmen in the world on the waters where the world's most prestigious regatta originated.

The spirit of sailing

The classic yachts' revival owes much to the beauty and elegance of the yachts at sea and the support and enthusiasm of their admirers on land.

173 The anchorage of Cala di Volpe, south of Porto Cervo in Sardinia, is famous for welcoming the most beautiful yachts in the world. On the evening this picture was taken, the triple-masted schooner *Shenandoah* (Ferris, 1902) and the former motor-yacht I*stria* lay at anchor, preferring to spend the night surrounded by the aromas of the Sardinian scrub rather than crowding into the tiny port, packed for the biennial *barca d'epoca* event. Like the classic yachts, many old motorboats have been recently restored and have their own particular venues, for example Monaco Classic Week. The ultimate achievement in this field would surely be to restore a steam yacht!

171 In high winds or calm weather, sailing close to the wind or in a fair wind, and regardless of owner, skipper or crew, *Altair* has always been and will remain a magnificent yacht, a model of perfection that dazzles those who are lucky enough to see her under sail. The two crew members perched on the end of the bow are wearing the type of clothing adopted by most classic-yacht crews – white overalls and bare feet, all the better to appreciate the feel of the teak decks!

175 The perfect lines of a huge sail gliding silently by, the soft autumn light and a diminutive figure, probably envying those lucky enough to be sailing on this great cruise-yacht … This is the type of unreal encounter that can be experienced at the great classic yacht events held in the Mediterranean. When you arrive, you never know what lies in store. Whether at sea or on land, the chance encounter of a few boats, a cloud and a ray of sunlight is enough to create the magical images and impressions that people come here to find.

The spirit of sailing

At Imperia, Monaco, Cannes and St Tropez, the spectacle of the classic yachts is always played out near the shore.

Distant
ports of call

As travelling becomes faster, simpler and easier, the feeling of having arrived at the ends of the earth has a very special savour all of its own. Fortunately, there are still many places on the planet, or at least on the sea, where you have the overwhelming impression of being so remote from everything that one more step will finally take you beyond the boundaries of the civilized world.

Getting to these places takes a good number of hours by air or days by sea. However, you're not actually that far from the South Pole if you find yourself in New Zealand or Patagonia, at the southernmost tip of the Pacific Ocean, where you have the delicious feeling of belonging more to the world of water and fish than of land and men. You begin to understand the enormous courage of the great maritime explorers who, throughout history, have continually pushed back the frontiers of the known world. You fully appreciate the nature of the difficulties encountered in these regions and realize just how much intelligence, determination and ingenuity they showed in overcoming the inadequacy of their ships and the unreliability of their equipment.

Patagonia is a truly fascinating place. You have the impression that you have wandered inadvertently into a world of giants, where the size of the serried ranks of mountainous waves that roll past Cape Horn, the force of the winds that roar down from the Andes, and the inhospitality of the mountains whose icy walls rise vertically from the sea far exceed anything to be experienced in more temperate zones. It is a universe in which man has no place, where nature flexes its muscles and demonstrates its strength as if to show what it is capable of if not treated with the respect it deserves.

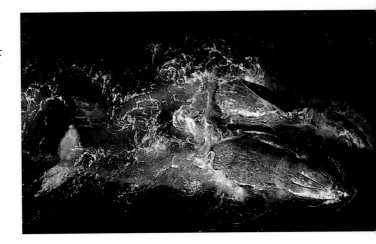

The splendour of inviolate nature in an anchorage nestling in the winding channels of Patagonia. Exploring the surrounding area is not as easy as it might appear since your feet sink into the peaty ground as if you were walking on fresh snow.
Dropping anchor in faraway places is an ideal opportunity for unexpected encounters with the real inhabitants of the ocean (above).

Distant ports of call

With its maze of dense, virgin vegetation, Marlborough Sound, between the two main islands of New Zealand, has all the appearance and wildness of the world

at the beginning of time. But the calm waters are deceptive. Here, when taking delivery
of a yacht built in Auckland, the first thing to do is to have it reinforced before setting sail.

Distant ports of call

Only cruise-yachts built to the highest specifications venture into the channels of Patagonia. This spectacular image shows the Garibaldi Glacier, which rises from the waters of the Beagle Channel, and *Shenandoah* on its

third round-the-world voyage, a fitting way to celebrate its centenary in 2002. Some places, like some boats, seem to remain untouched by the ravages of time.

Distant ports of call

Nugget Point, at the southern tip of New Zealand, marks the end of the
civilized world. Out there, on the open sea, there's nothing but

albatrosses, huge waves that sweep round the world without encountering
land, icebergs and, further still, the icy wastes of the Antarctic.

Under sail
Gilles Martin-Raget would like to thank

The owners and managers of the boats and yachts that sail on the sea, the designers who create them and the shipyards that build them, the captains and skippers who race and sail them, the crews, navigators and sailors under their command, the race organizers and all those who work with ships and the sea.

Those who bring the sea to life and gave rise to the images in this book – images that simply wouldn't have been possible without the help of the men and women who have given me their invaluable support, assistance and confidence, in particular:

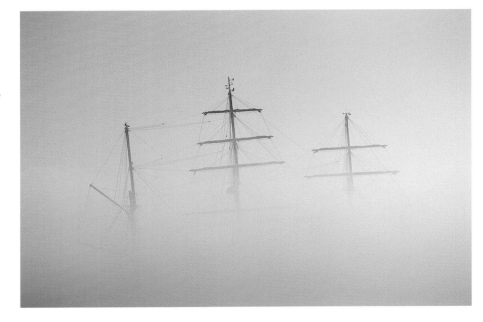

Gabrielle Abraham, Sophie Adde, Frédéric Alain, Bernard d'Alessandri, Daniel Allisy, Yves Anrys, Isabelle Andrieux, Félix Aubry de la Noë, Eric Augé, Christophe Auguin, Gérard de Ayala, Jean-René Bannwart, Luca Bassani, André Beaufils, Christine Bélanger, Hervé Borde, Vincent Borde, Carlo Borlenghi, Margherita Bottini, Dominic Bourgeois, Laurent Bourgnon, Bouygues Telecom, Lucien Boyer, Michel Buntz, Françoise Buntz Milliton, Patrick Buteux, Yves Carcelle, Patrice Carpentier, Martial Caspard, Catana, Laurent Célarié, Catherine Chabaud, François Chalain, Christian Chalmain, Daniel Charles, Xavier Chaubert, Paul Chiron, Pierre Chomarat, Patrice de Colmont, Anne Combier, Scott Coupé, Eric Coquerel, Corum, Jean-Michel Couve, Laurence Dacoury, Myriam Daman, Denis Delebecque, Michel Desjoyeaux, Chris Dickson, Noëlle Duck, Christian Dumard, Anne-Marie Dufetel, Gaelle Du Penhouat, Camille Elbeze, Pierre English, Laurent Esquier, Bénédicte Etienne, Philippe Facque, Roland Fardeau, la Fédération française de Voile, Pierre Fehlmann, Christian Février, Hélène de Fontainieu, Daniel Forster, Jean-François Fountaine, Pierre Fountaine, Foncia, Fujifilm France, Annie Fyot, Alain Gautier, William Garit, Luc Gelusseau, Geodis, Pierre Giboire, Daniel Gilles, Yvan Griboval, Dominique Guichard, François and Françoise Guiter, Havas sports, Klaus Hebben, Benoît Heimermann, Hervé Hillard, Marie-Laure Hermanche, Philippe Holder, Vincent Horeau, Marcus Hutchinson, Julia Huvé, Isabelle Jendron, Jour J, Ortwin Kandler, Stéphane Kandler, Kos Picture Source, Olivier Lafourcade, Pierre Lavialle,

Raymond Langlois, Flore Lecomte, Jacques Lehn, Patrick Leroux, Xavier de Lesquen, Jean-Marc Loubier, Daniel Manoury, Ellen Mac Arthur, Jacques, Nicole, Marie, Céline and Sylvie Martin-Raget, Maguelonne, Swann, Guilhem and Colin Martin-Raget, Lara Montel, Nautique, 9 Telecom, Daniel Nottet, Objectif Bastille, Jean-Pierre Odero, Orange, Eric Ogden, Bertrand Pacé, Serge Paillard, Marc Pajot, Yves Pajot, Monica Paolazzi, Mireille Paoli-Vatine, Jo and Françoise Pascal, Jean-Luc Paulou, Les Editions Pêcheur d'Images, Pascal Pellat-Finet, Philippe de Pennart, Emmanuel Perrault, Olivier Perretié, Eric Petit, Bruno Peyron, Loïck Peyron, Picto Marseille, Guillaume Plisson, Philip and Marie-Brigitte Plisson, Promovoile, Publicis Méditerranée, Erwan Quéméré, Didier Ravon, Dominique Romet, Alain Rondeau, Yves Rousset-Rouard, Annette Roux, Royale Production, François Salle, Jean-Pierre Salles, Sea and See, Sea and See Italia, La Société Nautique de Marseille, Kaoru Soehata, Jean-Michel Straussesein (+), Bertrand Suchet, Patrick Teboul, Jérôme Teigné, Alain Thébault, Bruno Troublé, Emmanuel de Toma, Mark Turner, L'Union Nationale pour la Course au Large, Luc le Vaillant, Monica Vianello, Bruno Voisart, Whirlpool France, and the editorial team and staff of *Voiles et Voiliers* magazine.

Editor Nathalie Bailleux
Designer Nancy Dorking
Graphics and production
Denis Delebecque
Copy editor Marie-Rose Lefèvre
Photoengraving
Flash Espace -Montpellier

First published by Hachette Livre (Éditions du Chêne)
© 2002 Hachette Livre (Éditions du Chêne)
This edition published by Hachette Illustrated UK, Octopus Publishing Group, 2–4 Heron Quays, London E14 4JP
© 2003 English translation, Octopus Publishing Group Ltd, London
English translation by JMS Books LLP

A CIP catalogue for this book is available from the British Library

ISBN: 1 84430 050 1

Printed in Singapore by Tien Wah Press

Gilles Martin-Raget can be contacted via his website: www.martin-raget.com